The
PULLMAN STRIKE

THE PULLMAN STRIKE OF 1894

TURNING POINT FOR AMERICAN LABOR

BY LINDA JACOBS ALTMAN

Spotlight on American History
The Millbrook Press • Brookfield, Connecticut

Cover photograph courtesy of The Granger Collection

Photographs courtesy of The Granger Collection: pp. 8, 15;
Library of Congress: pp. 12–13, 19, 25, 27 (both), 31, 33, 37,
39, 45, 52; Bettmann Archive: pp. 16, 21, 42, 48–49; Chicago
Historical Society: p. 23; Historic Pullman Foundation,
Chicago: pp. 28–29; UPI/Bettmann Newsphotos: p. 55.

Library of Congress Cataloging-in-Publication Data

Altman, Linda Jacobs. 1943–
The Pullman strike of 1894 : turning point for American
labor / by Linda Jacobs Altman.
p.   cm.—(Spotlight on American history)
Includes bibliographical references and index.
Summary: Discusses the people and events involved in the
unsuccessful but influential strike by railroad workers at the
Pullman Company in Chicago in 1894.
ISBN 1-56294-346-4 (lib. bdg.)
1. Chicago Strike, 1894—Juvenile literature. [1. Chicago
Strike, 1894. 2. Strikes and lockouts—Rail-
roads. 3. Railroads—History.] I. Title. II. Series.
HD5325.R12 1894.C5359 1994
331.89′282523′0977311—dc20   93-10880   CIP   AC

Published by The Millbrook Press
2 Old New Millford Road, Brookfield, Connecticut 06804

Contents

The
PULLMAN STRIKE

INTRODUCTION:
HARD TIMES

Times were bad in 1894. Factories and stores shut down. Farmers lost their land. Industrial workers lost their jobs. In May of that year, the Pullman Palace Car Company announced pay cuts for its three thousand workers.

In its factory near Chicago, Illinois, Pullman built luxury sleeping cars for the railroads. These cars had seats that opened up into beds, and upper berths that folded down from the walls. Although tickets for Pullman cars cost more than regular seats, hundreds gladly paid the price—until hard times made them think twice about spending money.

When business fell off, Pullman decided to reduce costs by cutting wages. The workers felt trapped. Not only did they work in the company factory, but they lived in the company town in company houses. Now they were making less money, but rent and other living expenses stayed the same.

While the workers struggled to get by, the company kept paying its stockholders (people who had bought shares of Pullman stock and expected to earn money on their investment). Even in this time of economic depression, the company continued to pay the stockholders. They called it good business. The workers called it unfair.

The workers at the Pullman Company decided to strike. They walked off their jobs and refused to go back to work until the company restored their lost wages. They knew that no single worker could force a big company like Pullman to raise wages or lower rents, but together they had a chance. That was the whole idea of a strike—workers banding together to do what none of them could do alone. They elected a strike committee to meet with management and try to reach an agreement.

The strike began in Chicago on May 11, 1894. On June 26, its effect spread through the nation's railway system when members of the American Railway Union joined the cause. Before it ended, the Pullman Strike would go down in history as a milestone of the American labor movement.

1

THE INDUSTRIAL REVOLUTION

America began as a nation of farmers. In 1790 almost four million people lived in the United States. Three and a quarter million of them lived on farms, sewed their own clothes, and made their own soap and candles, even furniture.

For things they couldn't do themselves, early Americans turned to local craftsmen and shopkeepers. Everything from wagons to leather shoes was made by hand, one item at a time.

Even work was different from what it is today. People didn't have jobs in the way we think of them now. They didn't commute back and forth to an office or earn a regular paycheck. People worked for themselves and lived where they worked—the farmer on his land, the craftsman in a little shop behind his house, the doctor in his study.

The Industrial Revolution in the nineteenth century changed all that. With the invention of the steam engine, things that used to be made by hand could be made by machine. Small shops gave way to giant factories and assembly lines. All over the country, people struggled, some more successfully than others, to adapt to the new ways.

During the nineteenth century's Industrial Revolution, giant factories sprang up all over the country, changing sleepy little towns into bustling cities.

It was a freewheeling time. Historians have named it the Gilded Age, after an 1873 novel by Mark Twain and Charles Dudley Warner about those land-grabbing, deal-making, fortune-building days of runaway growth. Instant millionaires flaunted, or showed off, their newfound wealth, with mansions and yachts, lavish gifts, and extravagant parties.

While the rich turned spending money into an art form, the middle class dreamed of following in their footsteps. Legions of would-be millionaires read the rags-to-riches tales of Horatio Alger. These books had titles like *Strive and Succeed* and *Making His Mark*. They promised that anybody who worked hard enough could rise to the top. A child born in a log cabin could grow up to be president. A simple farm boy could become a wealthy industrialist. It was a beautiful dream.

Powered by this dream of limitless growth, everything about America seemed fabulous. People flocked to see P. T. Barnum's circus and Buffalo Bill's Wild West show. Baseball became the national pastime, and every town had its vaudeville theater.

Thanks to the railroads, American industry developed with dizzying speed. Trains were the lifeline of every factory town. They brought raw materials in and hauled finished goods out. By 1894 the transcontinental railroad was twenty-five years old. It had become such a part of the American scene that people could hardly imagine life without it.

The railroad began as the fanciful idea of men like American inventor Oliver Evans, who talked about "carriages propelled by steam" that would travel at the unthinkable rate of 300 miles (480 kilometers) a day. Somewhat later, he got the notion of running these steam-powered carriages on wooden rails.

Not many people listened to Evans. After all, the man seemed very strange. In 1804 he built the first steam-powered vehicle in

Wealthy industrialists, having made millions from the railroads, flaunted their fortunes with luxuries like this summer home in Newport, Rhode Island.

America. He called it a dredge. It was an odd-looking thing—part wagon, part boat. It belched smoke and sparks and made a mighty racket. People looked and laughed. In 1804 nobody dreamed that great steam locomotives would soon travel over a system of rails that spanned the continent.

It took men of vision to imagine such a thing, but it took men of business to get down to the nuts-and-bolts reality of building it. Many of these industrialists didn't know the first thing about laying track or building locomotives. They just knew how to make money.

*A railroad construction crew in 1885. The railroads paid
practically nothing for long hours of hard labor.*

Some people called them captains of industry. Others called them robber barons or moguls (powerful or important people). To build the railroads, the moguls needed land and a ready source of cheap labor.

The land came from government grants. To encourage railroads to build new lines, the government gave them huge tracts of land free of charge. They could develop part of it, and sell the rest to raise money for even more expansion.

For their labor force, the railroads needed people who would work long hours for low pay and not complain about conditions. They hired freed slaves from the southern United States, along with immigrants from foreign countries.

Nobody thought of these workers as human beings. The moguls would have laughed at the idea of pension funds to provide for the workers' retirement and unemployment insurance to pay them in case of layoffs. The workers themselves didn't expect such things.

After all, no one intended to lay railroad track forever, or to work at a factory for a lifetime. The low-paying drudgery was only a stepping-stone to bigger and better things. For some, that was true; for others, only a dream. The factory, the mine, and the railroad yards became a grim, lifelong reality for many Americans.

2

THE AMERICAN WORKER

Faced with the hard realities of industrialization, workers began banding together to demand better wages and working conditions. The American labor movement was born.

As workers explored the power of group action, they soon learned that railroads made ideal targets for strikes and boycotts. The whole of American industry depended on a healthy and efficient railway system. Anything that stopped the trains, or slowed them down, would send shock waves all over the country.

In 1877 a stunned America saw how quickly labor unrest could cripple the nation's trains. Workers at the Baltimore and Ohio Railroad walked off their jobs when the company announced new pay cuts.

No union organized this walkout; no strike committee voted for it. It just happened. In Martinsburg, West Virginia, and in Baltimore, Maryland, angry strikers fought with soldiers and police.

The strike spread to the Pennsylvania Railroad. It didn't take long for trouble to start. Mobs of workers destroyed the railroad yards. They tore up track, smashed cars, and set fire to the Union Depot. A thousand federal troops were called in to restore order.

The violence that suddenly erupted during
the 1877 Baltimore & Ohio Railroad strike
shocked the nation, but it turned out to be
only the beginning of weeks of rioting.

Rioting spread to Boston, Chicago, and Buffalo. In two weeks, more than one hundred people died and at least five hundred were injured. When the dust settled, many workers were fired outright; the lucky few who kept their jobs went back to work at the same old wage.

Jobs and pay raises weren't all that the workers lost in those violent days of 1877; they also lost the sympathy and support of the American public. At the beginning, many people had sided with the workers. Then riots and killings showed a new and frightening side of labor unrest. Nobody liked what they saw. Newspapers denounced the violence, businessmen denounced the workers, and politicians promised that such a thing would never happen again.

Only a few people looked beyond the riots to the underlying causes of labor unrest. They saw what America's leaders didn't want to see: that the uprising of 1877 was only the beginning. The struggle between management and labor was likely to get worse before it got better.

Factory workers didn't have the bargaining power of skilled craftsmen (people who had special training for their work). Assembly lines and freight yards were full of people with strong backs and no training. In the new world of steam engines and giant factories, these workers were considered disposable.

Nobody realized that more sharply than the founders of the American Federation of Labor (AFL). The AFL was formed in 1886. Samuel Gompers of the Cigar Makers Union became the first president, with Peter J. McGuire of the Brotherhood of Carpenters as secretary. The AFL's goal was to organize small trade unions into an effective national organization. Its founders vowed "to protect the skilled labor of America . . . and to sustain the standard of American workmanship and skill."

Samuel Gompers, one of the founders of the American Federation of Labor and its first president.

The AFL reached out to trained craftsmen like printers, carpenters, bricklayers, and bakers. They didn't even try to organize the thousands of unskilled workers who toiled in America's factories, doing jobs that a thousand other people could easily learn to do.

By twentieth-century standards, that may sound cold and heartless. By nineteenth-century standards, it was only realistic. The skill of its members was a union's only bargaining chip. Unskilled workers couldn't hope to win a strike in those early days of industrialization.

But a group called the Knights of Labor did try to organize skilled and unskilled workers into a single national union. Although their strikes against several railroads in the 1880s were reasonably successful, by 1893 the Knights of Labor had fallen apart, leaving thousands of angry unskilled workers with nowhere to turn.

The 1886 riot at Chicago's Haymarket Square and the 1892 steel strike in Homestead, Pennsylvania, had a lot in common with the Pullman Strike. Many historians group them together: Haymarket, Homestead, Pullman. Haymarket started as a protest rally and ended as a tragedy. The people who gathered on May 4, 1886, weren't on strike and they weren't looking for trouble. They were there to condemn the shooting of workers during a strike against the McCormick Harvester company.

A number of known anarchists (people who want to abolish all forms of organized government) attended the meeting. Some of them spoke to the crowd while others passed out leaflets. Anarchists were not the most popular people in Chicago. Many civic leaders thought they were dangerous, or crazy, or both. The police decided to break up the rally before it turned ugly.

People were leaving peacefully when somebody tossed a bomb into police lines. Instantly, the rally became a full-scale riot. Seven

Attention Workingmen!

GREAT

MASS-MEETING

TO-NIGHT, at 7.30 o'clock,

AT THE

HAYMARKET, Randolph St., Bet. Desplaines and Halsted.

Good Speakers will be present to denounce the latest atrocious act of the police, the shooting of our fellow-workmen yesterday afternoon.

THE EXECUTIVE COMMITTEE.

policemen and four demonstrators died as a result of the violence at Haymarket Square.

The police rounded up every anarchist leader they could find. The police never did identify who actually threw the bomb, but that didn't seem to matter. A shocked public demanded that someone pay for the outrages at Haymarket Square. Eight men were arrested and stood trial for murder. Four of the eight were hanged. A fifth took his own life. The remaining three were eventually pardoned and released from prison.

[23]

Another strike, this one in 1892, pitted workers against the vast empire of the Carnegie Steel Company. It began when the company announced pay cuts of up to 26 percent. The workers at the Carnegie plant in Homestead, Pennsylvania, called a strike, although they knew from the start that it wouldn't be easy to win. Practically everyone in Homestead worked for Carnegie Steel. Times would be very hard with so many out of work. The men got ready for a long struggle.

Andrew Carnegie, an owner, was vacationing in England when the strike began. His partner Henry Frick was in charge of the plant. Frick wasn't a man to sit around and wait for trouble to come to him. Several days before the workers actually walked off their jobs, he contacted the famous Pinkerton Detective Agency and hired his own private army.

The Carnegie Steel plant closed down on July 2. By July 5, a force of three hundred Pinkertons assembled in Pittsburgh. The plan was for the detectives to slip into Homestead after dark.

Somehow the strikers got wind of the plan. They were ready and waiting when the Pinkertons arrived at dawn on July 6. What had been a peaceful labor dispute exploded into an armed conflict. Several people were killed and many were injured.

Although by this time Andrew Carnegie had cabled Frick from England to "stand firm," it was a battle that Mr. Frick's private army couldn't win. The strikers were defending their homes and families. The Pinkertons were only earning a paycheck. By late afternoon they were soon forced to retreat, leaving the jubilant workers to celebrate their victory.

Too late they learned that winning this battle had cost them the war with Carnegie Steel. The defeat of the Pinkertons convinced Pennsylvania governor Robert Pattison that things were get-

The retreat of the Pinkertons at Homestead, Pennsylvania,
was only a brief victory for the Carnegie Steel workers.
Days later the Pennsylvania state militia arrived, and
the strike at Carnegie Steel was broken.

ting out of hand. On July 12 troops entered Homestead, and within hours the state militia controlled the streets and the strike was broken (ended by force). Some of the strikers quit their jobs, but most went back to work at the lower wage.

3

LIVING THE
PULLMAN WAY

George Mortimer Pullman was an American original: part inventor, part natural-born mogul. He had good ideas and a knack for being in the right place at the right time. It was a knack that made him rich and famous. George Pullman put his stamp on everything he touched—the sleeping car he designed, the company he founded, the workers he tried to control.

Pullman didn't invent the railroad sleeping car—he refined it. The idea had been around since 1829, but aside from a brief trial on the Erie Railroad, it hadn't caught on with the public.

George Pullman was sure he could build a better sleeping car, one that railroads would use and passengers would love. He talked the Chicago & Alton Railroad into giving him two old cars to convert into sleepers.

On September 1, 1858, one of those cars made its first run. George Pullman was on hand to oversee every detail. He even hired his own conductor rather than turn his pride and joy over to the regular Alton staff.

That first trip set a tone for the future. Pullman didn't sell his cars to railroads. He leased them, fully stocked and fully staffed.

A *Pullman palace car and its staff. George Pullman (inset) prided himself on his absolute control over every detail of his business.*

He made rules and regulations for everything, right down to the number of sheets and towels each car should carry. The Pullman Palace Car Company thrived. In the company shops and yards, hundreds of workers turned out dozens of new cars each year.

In 1881, George Pullman founded the town that bore his name—Pullman, Illinois. He built it the same way he built his first sleeping cars, with personal attention to every detail. When the streets and houses, churches, schools, and stores met with his approval, he populated the town by making a new rule: All Pullman workers were required to live in the company town.

The outside world hailed Pullman, Illinois, as a model of planned communities. Everything was neat and clean, from the brick row houses where people lived to the manicured park where their children played.

George Pullman was enormously proud of the town he had created. He ruled it like an uncrowned king, never doubting that his way was best for everyone. He decided how much to pay his employees for their work and how much to charge them for rent. Pullman owned every store in town, plus all the public utilities. Even sewage was recycled to use as fertilizer on the Pullman farm.

A view of Pullman, Illinois, shows the workers' row houses in front, with dormitory-type housing for unmarried men behind.

MR. PULLMAN'S PALACE

ALTHOUGH THE FIRST TRAINS were faster than wagons or stagecoaches, they were not necessarily safer or more comfortable. The steam boilers on early locomotives had a nasty habit of exploding when they became overheated. Derailings were common because tracks had too many sharp, flat curves. Even when the train stayed on the tracks, the ride was rough. Passenger cars were boxes on wheels with no shock absorbers to soften the ride. Every so often the train took a curve too fast and dumped everybody on the floor. Occasionally trains came screeching to a halt because a herd of cattle or even buffalo had wandered onto the tracks.

When they weren't being thrown about, passengers sat on hard wooden benches. In summer they gagged on the smoke and dust that poured through the open windows. In winter they huddled around a wood stove in the middle of the car.

Every now and again, sparks would set the car on fire, sending frantic passengers scurrying for water to put out the flames.

In this rugged and dangerous world, George Pullman's lavish rolling palaces were a revolution in comfort. The first car he built cost over twenty thousand dollars of his own money. He named it *Pioneer*.

The car was so elegant and grand that it stunned everyone who saw it. Its undercarriage was cushioned with blocks of solid rubber for a smoother ride. Its interior was like a fancy drawing room, with plush carpets, carved woodwork, and mirrors in solid brass frames. By night, upper and lower berths acted as bunk beds. By day, the lower berth became a sitting couch. The upper berth folded up against the ceiling on a specially designed hinge.

There was just one problem with *Pioneer:* It was too tall to fit through railroad tunnels

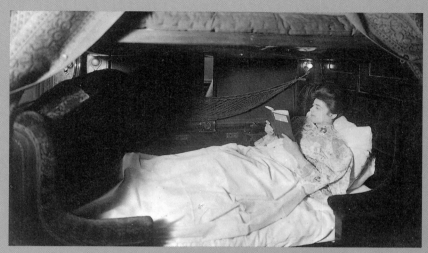

Sleeping berths on a Pullman palace car

and too wide to get past depot platforms. The railroad companies weren't willing to re-build all their facilities for an experimental coach.

That could have been the end of the Pullman sleeper car if not for Abraham Lincoln's funeral train. The President's widow, Mary Todd Lincoln, asked to have the elegant new Pullman car on the train that would take her husband's body back to Springfield, Illinois, for burial.

So carpenters and bridge builders went to work, making the necessary changes. As the train bearing the slain President's body moved across the country, many people got their first glimpse of the *Pioneer*.

Suddenly it seemed everybody wanted to travel in a Pullman sleeper. The railroads changed their tunnels and platforms, and George Pullman went into the business that would soon make his name a household word.

The town grew and appeared to prosper. George Pullman liked to think of himself as the beloved benefactor of 12,000 happy people. His town provided for them from the cradle to the grave. It served as an example to other industries all over the country. In 1889 the American Bar Association held its annual meeting in Chicago. A highlight of the event was a tour of this "workers' paradise."

Five years later, the paradise fell apart.

The depression of 1893 hit the Pullman Palace Car Company hard. Americans were traveling less and watching their expenses more carefully. Poor people had never been able to afford the extra fare for a sleeping car; in the leaner economy of 1894, the well-to-do couldn't afford it either. When ticket sales dropped, the railroads stopped ordering new Pullmans.

To get through the emergency, Pullman cut back production, laying off almost half of its workers. Those who kept their jobs faced an average pay cut of 25 percent.

While wages plunged, the workers' living expenses didn't budge. Groceries from the company store and rent on company housing cost as much as ever. One man worked 120 hours and got a check for seven cents. That was all he had left after the company deducted his rent and expenses.

During the winter of 1893–1894, children missed school because they had no shoes or warm clothing to wear. Families went hungry because they couldn't afford groceries at the company store.

The company ignored this human misery. It was, after all, good business to cut expenses during a depression. It was not good business to cut rents. Mr. Pullman had gone to the time and trouble to build the town; he felt it was up to the workers to make it self-supporting.

This photograph, taken on the shore of Lake Michigan near
Chicago during the depression of 1893, shows men and boys
scavenging for scraps of food, wood, or anything they could sell.

While the company held firm with the employees, it paid a whopping 8 percent dividend to its shareholders. By the spring of 1894, the workers were not only desperate, they were angry. They chose a committee to meet with Mr. Pullman.

Reading from a prepared statement, Pullman simply restated his determination to cut costs by lowering wages.

Moguls of the Gilded Age didn't like questions or demands from their employees. They wanted complete obedience. A worker who dared to complain was apt to be fired on the spot. That was simply the way things were. In refusing to consider the employees' demands, George Pullman thought he had settled the matter once and for all.

He was wrong.

4

THE STRIKE BEGINS

*O*n *May 11, 1894*, three thousand Pullman Palace Car Company workers walked off their jobs. George Pullman was furious. He promptly closed down the shops, leaving the remaining three hundred workers, who had remained loyal to him, without jobs.

Many of the strikers belonged to the new American Railway Union (ARU), founded by a man named Eugene V. Debs. They turned to him for advice.

Debs understood the problem all too well. He had quit school at the age of fourteen to work in the railroad shops. After taking a job with a grocer and serving several terms as city clerk of his hometown of Terre Haute, Indiana, Debs returned to the railroad industry. As a fireman for the railroads, Debs became aware of the quiet misery of his fellow laborers.

He saw hardworking men with worn faces who toiled for low wages. He saw many of them injured or even killed because of unsafe equipment—boilers that exploded, bridges that collapsed, rails that wore out. The workers accepted these dangers as just another part of the job.

Debs couldn't do that.

He set out to make things better, not just for himself but for everyone. After helping to start the American Railway Union, Debs built it to 150,000 members in a few short months. The union was open to skilled and unskilled railroad employees. Debs believed that industry-wide organizations could help workers better than the craft unions favored by Samuel Gompers and the AFL.

In April 1894, Debs put his idea to the test with a strike against the Great Northern Railway. Great Northern had cut wages three times in less than a year. Highly skilled engineers and conductors earned only eighty dollars a month. Ordinary laborers made ten cents an hour.

Debs demanded a raise for his members. When the company refused, he called a strike. For eighteen days, the Great Northern was paralyzed. Freight piled up on the loading docks. Passenger coaches stood empty on the siderails.

The only thing that moved was the U.S. Mail. If the mail stopped, the government would send troops to get it started again. That could break the strike in no time, and Debs was determined not to let that happen.

Great Northern finally gave in and offered a raise—sixteen dollars a month for most employees. Happy strikers went back to work. In all of American history, this was the first real victory for a railroad union.

Eugene Debs became an overnight hero to working people all over the country. When the Pullman workers came to him for help, Debs didn't turn them away. He went to Pullman town to see conditions for himself. He was shocked by what he found. Like most people in the country, Debs had heard high praise for George Pullman's model village. The homes and stores and streets were nice enough, but most of the people didn't have enough to eat.

Eugene V. Debs, founder of the American Rail-way Union and organizer of the Pullman Strike.

Debs couldn't turn away from the people of Pullman. He invited them to attend the first national convention of the American Railway Union, which was coming up in June. They came gladly and told the entire convention about how they worked and lived. The delegates wanted to support them with a boycott: They would refuse to move any train with a Pullman car attached.

But Debs wasn't ready for such a big move. He understood the members' feelings, but he also understood the risks and hardships of a major boycott. He convinced the membership to try a softer approach first. A committee would ask to meet with Pullman officials. They would request that both sides agree to submit the matter for arbitration (settlement by someone who listens to both sides and makes a decision).

It sounded like a good idea until the committee made a formal request to meet with Pullman management. Not only did the company reject the very idea of arbitration, but managers wouldn't even agree to meet with union representatives.

George Pullman was a stubborn, unyielding man who was offended that "his people," as he called them, would dare to question any rule he saw fit to make. Arbitration was out of the question, because in his mind there was nothing to arbitrate.

In the face of this rigid stubbornness, Eugene Debs gave up hope of settling the issues in a friendly manner. On June 15 the ARU membership listened to Debs tell of his failed effort to meet with officials at the Pullman Company. After due consideration, they voted to boycott beginning on June 26.

The battle with Pullman began.

Eugene Debs rolled up his sleeves and set to work. The first order of business was keeping federal troops out of Chicago. That meant no violence and no damage to railroad property. It meant

An illustration that appeared in Harper's Weekly *during the first days of the Pullman Strike shows the stopped trains at the Chicago & Northwestern Railroad yard.*

making sure the mail got through safely and on time, since nothing could bring down the full fury of the government faster than a threat to the U.S. Mail. Debs gave the orders loud and clear: Keep the mails moving and the Pullman cars sitting on a sidetrack.

The railroads handled the strike through an organization called the General Managers Association. They took a hard line against the boycott: Nobody had the right to tell them whom to hire, whom to fire, or how much they ought to pay.

The twenty-four railroads of the General Managers Association moved quickly to put down the strike. They announced that any switchman who refused to handle Pullman cars would be fired on the spot. The union countered with an announcement of its own: If a worker was fired for honoring the boycott, every union man in that yard would walk off the job.

The plan snowballed. In less than twenty-four hours, 5,000 men had laid down their tools and quit. By June 29 the number had grown to almost 50,000. Crowds of strike supporters began stopping trains. Soon all rail traffic west of Chicago was at a standstill. Here and there, fights broke out. The city of Chicago held its breath. People felt like they were living on top of a powder keg that could explode at any minute.

Nobody had expected the workers to hold out for so long. The railroads vowed to break the strike at all costs. Since their own men hadn't been able to do it, they needed the help of government troops. Getting them wasn't going to be easy.

5

THE BATTLE
FOR CHICAGO

The only way the railroads could get assistance from the government to break the Pullman Strike would be if the president of the United States stepped in. And President Grover Cleveland had a firm policy: He would not send federal troops to control a strike unless a state governor asked for them.

This was a problem for the Pullman General Managers Association. Governor John P. Altgeld of Illinois would never ask for troops. Altgeld was a liberal with a lifelong sympathy for the underdog. The wealthy and powerful saw him as a threat to everything they held dear. The governor believed that the rights of working people were just as important as the rights of their bosses. Ideas like that made the railroads nervous.

One of Altgeld's acts as governor had been to pardon the three Haymarket anarchists who were still in the state prison. This was not a popular decision, but the new governor was a man of strong beliefs.

With one stroke of the pen, he had proved that he wasn't afraid to take unpopular positions. If he would free the dreaded anarchists, who openly favored rebellion against the government,

This sketch captures the rage felt by striking railroad workers as they attacked strikebreakers (scabs) who took jobs as brakemen and switchmen during the strike.

there was no telling what he might do about the Pullman Strike. The railroads couldn't afford to wait and see.

The railroad managers flooded the newspapers with stories that painted the American Railway Union as a lawless gang and Eugene Debs as a wild-eyed radical. Again and again, they reminded the American public of Haymarket and Homestead. Labor unrest had always meant violence and mayhem. There was no reason to believe it would be different this time.

To keep the strikers off balance, the railroads began attaching Pullman cars to everything that moved—even freight trains that carried no passengers at all. They made plans to hire strikebreakers, who would work at low pay, keep their mouths shut, and do as they were told.

Finding applicants wouldn't be difficult; protecting them while they worked might be a problem. But, in 1894, being a strikebreaker was not the shameful thing it has come to be in modern times. The labor movement was new, and was making up the rules as it went along. It would take years before "scab!" and "strikebreaker!" became terrible insults.

The General Managers Association was worried. They feared this upstart union just might pull off the biggest upset in railroad history. And, in fact, it might have worked out that way if it had not been for U.S. attorney general Richard Olney.

Olney was a stern and stubborn man who liked simple answers to difficult questions. Before joining President Cleveland's administration, he had been a successful lawyer for half a dozen railroads. Even after he became attorney general, he continued as a consultant for the Chicago, Burlington & Quincy Railroad. Olney didn't see any conflict of interest in this unusual arrangement. To his way of thinking, there was no real difference between working for a government and working for a railroad. Together they represented established authority.

Olney never saw the Pullman Strike as an honest dispute between management and labor. He didn't try to consider both sides for the simple reason that he didn't think the workers even had a side. As owners, the railroad companies had the right to do whatever they wanted with their property. Workers could always quit if they didn't like the wages or working conditions. To the attorney general of the United States, it was just that simple.

When the General Managers Association asked for help, Richard Olney gave it gladly. He appointed a railroad lawyer named Edwin Walker to serve as special U.S. attorney for the strike. From the beginning, the two men worked closely together, looking for a way to end the strike.

In the rail yards of Chicago, nothing moved. All around the country, transportation slowed down or stopped.

Then came Blue Island.

On June 29, Eugene Debs visited this little town, just 16 miles (26 kilometers) south of Chicago. In a stirring speech, he asked the railroad workers of Blue Island to support the Pullman boycott. The support he got was not the kind he wanted.

The workers of Blue Island were already spoiling for a fight. They wanted to do more than support the Pullman boycott. They wanted to send their own bosses an unforgettable message. The day after Debs made his speech, a switchman purposely derailed a locomotive in the middle of the main track. That one act of defiance triggered an uprising. Angry workers destroyed the yards and set fire to anything that moved. They fought with deputy marshals who came to restore order.

The destruction of the trains and railway yards at the town of Blue Island infuriated the Illinois attorney general. He demanded help from the government.

When the smoke cleared, Attorney General Olney had the evidence he needed to get the government involved. On July 2, he got an injunction (a legal order from a court) against the strike. Under this order, strike leaders couldn't even talk about the boycott. Any railroad worker who walked off the job or refused to perform any of his normal duties was guilty of a crime.

It was one of the most sweeping injunctions in American history. The attorney general knew it could never be enforced, but that was just what he had in mind. He went straight to President Cleveland and asked him to send federal troops into Chicago. Olney claimed that the strike was unlawful and dangerous. It should be crushed without mercy.

The President wasn't sure of the constitutional grounds. Neither the mayor of Chicago nor the governor of Illinois had asked for federal help. There was no national emergency. Could an American president send troops anyway? Grover Cleveland wasn't sure. One clause in the Constitution seemed to say yes; another seemed to say no.

While the President sorted things out, Eugene Debs faced a decision of his own: what to do about the injunction. Ignoring it would probably land him in jail, but obeying it meant giving up the strike. He could not bring himself to do that.

Debs and his people continued the boycott. The attorney general notified Washington that local authorities needed assistance: He was asking for troops. For extra insurance, Olney got a federal judge and a U.S. marshal to sign the statement. He presented it at the July 3 meeting of the President's cabinet.

On the strength of that statement, the cabinet advised President Cleveland to send troops into Chicago. The Pullman Strike was more than an ordinary labor dispute, they said. It was turning into an all-out war that endangered the mails, and might even threaten national security.

On July 4, 1894, by order of the President of the United States, federal troops entered the city of Chicago. It was the first time any president had done such a thing on his own authority. President Rutherford B. Hayes did it during the "Great Strike" of 1877, but only after the governor of West Virginia asked for help.

Illinois governor Altgeld had not asked. When the troops came anyway, he protested bitterly, but nothing he said could change what had been done or stop what was about to happen.

United States soldiers patrolled the streets of Chicago. More than three thousand deputy marshals worked with them. These special deputies weren't trained soldiers. They were men who were in need of work, or who simply enjoyed a good fight. Some had arrest records for crimes like theft, brawling, or public drunkenness. The General Managers Association recruited them and paid for their services.

That made the strikers angrier than ever. It was only a matter of time before violence broke out, and the railroads were ready to use that to their own advantage.

Just breaking the strike wasn't enough for the managers, however. Against tremendous odds, a band of unskilled laborers had brought the mighty railroads to a standstill. Along the way, the workers had gained a sense of their own power. That could mean strike after strike after costly strike. To take back control of their companies, the managers had to break the union. Violence in the streets played right into their hands.

By July 6 the city of Chicago looked like a war zone. Rioters ran wild in the streets, stopping trains, smashing switches, setting fire to anything that would burn. The next day another mob attacked soldiers who were escorting a train through downtown Chicago. By the time the shooting stopped, several people lay dead and many more were wounded.

President Cleveland issued an order forbidding "unlawful assemblies" in the riot zones. That allowed the soldiers to break up small gatherings before they got big enough to be dangerous. To enforce these strict new measures, the president sent more troops into the city.

While all of this was going on, Governor Altgeld and Chicago mayor John P. Hopkins continued to protest. They complained to the President, the courts, the Congress—anyone who might listen. Nobody did.

Federal troops, authorized by President Cleveland, fire on the strikers in an attempt to control rioting.

The Pullman Strike was already bringing back memories of earlier labor revolts that began as strikes and ended as small-scale wars. Slowly but surely, public sympathy turned against the striking workers.

On July 10, Eugene Debs and three other union leaders were arrested for interfering with the U.S. Mail. Although they were released after a few hours, Debs realized that the strike was a lost cause. To salvage something for ARU members, he turned to Samuel Gompers of the AFL. Gompers had never supported the boycott because he disliked ARU's open membership policy. He still didn't believe that an industry-wide union could hope to succeed.

But Debs still thought that Gompers was the man to approach the railroad owners with a simple and straightforward offer: ARU would call off the boycott if the railroads would agree to rehire the union's members. When Gompers refused to get involved, it was the beginning of the end.

With no one to help them, and the troops breathing down their necks, the strikers couldn't keep up the struggle. Tired, hungry and battle-weary, many of them drifted back to the same old jobs at the same old pay. They had to sign employment contracts promising not to join any union, ever again.

Others couldn't go back. They were fired and their names were put on a "blacklist." No railroad in the country would hire a man whose name appeared on that list.

By July 17, Eugene Debs was back in jail. This time the charge was contempt of court, for disobeying the antistrike injunction of July 2. He was convicted and sentenced to six months in jail.

Debs also faced trial for conspiracy to obstruct a mail train. On this second charge, he was defended by a rising young attorney named Clarence Darrow.

Darrow was smart and idealistic. He built a strong case for his client, so strong that it looked like he would win. Then one of the jurors became ill, and the judge postponed the trial. It was never resumed.

Debs had to serve the full six months on the contempt conviction. By the time he got out of jail, the union he had worked so hard to build was dead. But Debs himself had become a living legend. On the day he was released from prison, ten thousand people gathered to cheer him when he walked through the gates.

When he got back to Chicago, more crowds cheered him. It didn't seem to matter that the Pullman boycott had been a costly failure, or that the union was dead. In the eyes of workers all over the country, Eugene Debs stood for the hopes and dreams of ordinary men.

George Pullman, owner of the Pullman Palace Car Company, came to stand for the greed and intolerance of the super-rich. On November 14, 1894, a special commission finished investigating the Pullman Strike. The commission's final report contained 681 pages of testimony and a 42-page summary. The report criticized U.S. attorney general Richard Olney and the General Managers Association, but laid the largest share of blame right on the doorstep of George Mortimer Pullman.

Before the strike, George Pullman had been admired as an enlightened employer who took care of his workers. After the strike, he was criticized for being greedy, high-handed, and unreasonable.

Of course, George Pullman didn't see it that way. He was hurt by what he saw as ingratitude from the workers. Perhaps he overheard some of the grim jokes they made about being baptized in a Pullman church, educated in a Pullman school, and sent when they died to a Pullman heaven or a Pullman hell.

DARROW FOR THE DEFENSE

CLARENCE DARROW was one of the most famous trial attorneys in American history. He had a clever mind, a ready wit, and a tongue sharp enough to cut prosecutors to shreds.

Darrow's effectiveness in court was only partly due to these qualities of mind; the rest was heart. He believed that there was no greater calling than to serve the cause of justice and human rights.

His formal schooling in the law was limited to one year at the University of Michigan, where he was not a particularly outstanding student. He did pass his bar examination, however, and set up practice in his hometown of Kinsman, Ohio. In 1887 he moved to Chicago, eager to tackle the burning issues of the time. He built a reputation as a fine trial attorney and earned the respect of his colleagues in the Chicago legal community.

It was the Debs case that brought him national fame as a

Clarence Darrow

defender of odd and often unpopular cases. Thirty-one years later, in 1925, Darrow went to Dayton, Tennessee, to defend teacher John T. Scopes. Scopes had been arrested for teaching the theory of evolution in public schools. Darrow's confrontation with fundamentalist politician William Jennings Bryan brought national attention to the now famous Scopes "monkey trials."

The company was his, after all, and so was the town. For years he had run them both, seeing to every detail. He simply couldn't understand why anybody would resent him for that.

After the strike George Pullman had another rude shock: The people of Pullman, Illinois, voted to make their town a part of Chicago. The mayor and city council of America's second-largest city took over the reins of government.

George Pullman was not a forgiving man. He became secretive and suspicious, constantly worried that someone would take what rightfully belonged to him. Shortly before his death in 1897, he ordered his grave lined in solid concrete so that looters couldn't rob him.

6

THE PULLMAN LEGACY

In the short run, the Pullman Strike was a costly failure for both sides: George Pullman lost his reputation as an enlightened businessman, and the railroads suffered millions of dollars' worth of damages. Eugene Debs ended up in prison, and hundreds of workers were worse off after the strike than they had been before.

The strike of 1894 raised issues that would define the labor struggle for years to come. It expanded the powers of the presidency, turned the court injunction into a weapon for industrial warfare, and let American business know that the gilded age of cheap labor and runaway growth was about to come to an end.

The troops that President Grover Cleveland had sent into Chicago on July 4 caused a storm of protest. Many people thought he had overstepped his authority. Governor Altgeld accused him of invading the sovereign state of Illinois. The investigating committee said he did the right thing. By the time the strike was over, the President had new freedom to act in times of national crisis, and so did the courts. The power given to the courts was the development that worried labor leaders most of all. By signing the injunction, the judge had made strikers into criminals and paved the way for federal troops to be called in strike situations.

*Congressional legislation now protects a union's
right to organize and picket and limits management's
ability to simply fire those who protest.*

The railroads called the Pullman injunction a "Gatling gun [machine gun] on paper." Labor unions called it "government by injunction." It had the force of law without the checks and balances of the democratic process. Even Samuel Gompers of the AFL was compelled to come forward and take a stand on this issue.

Gompers wasn't a political man. He didn't want to seek public office or form a labor party to run against the Republicans and the Democrats. All he wanted from government was the freedom to organize, strike, and boycott in support of labor's rights. He opposed "government by injunction" because it interfered with those rights.

Under Gompers's leadership the AFL continued to press for laws protecting the rights of labor. Gompers tried to work with management, hoping to win small gains for his members without risking everything on a strike they couldn't hope to win.

It was a long struggle. But now at least government commissions and committees treated labor unrest with new seriousness. Responsible people looked long and hard at the dangers of government by court injunction and presidential decree.

Finally, in 1914, Congress passed a law that limited the use of injunctions in labor disputes and affirmed a union's right to organize and picket. Other legislation followed as Congress and the newly formed Department of Labor groped their way toward a national labor policy.

Even in failure, the Pullman Strike had served notice on those who wanted to solve new problems with old methods. The message was straightforward and clear: The strike was over, but the struggle for fair treatment and decent wages had only just begun.

Chronology

May 11, 1894   Pullman Palace Car Company workers walk off their jobs to protest wage cuts.

June 21   Members of the American Railway Union vote to support the strike by refusing to handle any Pullman cars beginning June 26.

June 26   The boycott begins at noon.

June 29   Debs speaks to workers in Blue Island, asking them to honor the boycott.

June 30   Angry Blue Island workers destroy railroad property.

July 2   A federal court issues an injunction against the strike.

July 4   Federal troops arrive in Chicago by order of President Grover Cleveland.

July 10   Eugene Debs arrested for obstructing the mails. Released within hours.

July 11   Boycott collapses. Trains begin to move again.

July 12   Debs meets with Samuel Gompers to ask for his help.

July 17   Debs is arrested again, this time for defying the injunction of July 2.

November 14   Special investigating commission releases its report on the Pullman Strike. The report is highly critical of George Pullman and his management.

Further Reading

American Heritage. *Railroads in the Days of Steam*. New York: American Heritage Publishing Company, 1960.

Cook, F. P. *The American Struggle: The Story of the Continuing Conflict Between Labor and Management*. New York: Doubleday and Company, 1974.

Douglas, George H. *All Aboard: The Railroad in American Life*. New York: Paragon Press, 1992.

Flatley, Dennis R. *The Railroads: Opening the West*. New York: Franklin Watts, 1989.

Gunston, Bill. *Railroads*. New York: Franklin Watts, 1988.

McKissack, Patricia and Fredrick. *A Long Hard Journey: The Story of the Pullman Porter*. New York: Walker and Company, 1990.

Scott, Geoffrey. *Labor Day*. Minneapolis: Carolrhoda Books, 1992.

Wetterer, Margaret K. *Kate Shelley and the Midnight Express*. Minneapolis: Carolrhoda Books, 1992.

Sources

Sources for *The Pullman Strike of 1894: Turning Point for American Labor* include reference books, histories, and biographies. Various organizations gave assistance and research materials for this project. The AFL/CIO and the U.S. Department of Labor furnished historical data on labor history, while the California State Railroad Museum Library and the Museum of Science and Industry supplied data on the Pullman Palace Cars. The Illinois State Historical Library was a valuable resource for biographical data on the people involved in the strike, and also supplied information on Chicago, Blue Island, and Pullman town.

A list of published sources follows:

Adams, James Truslow. *Album of American History: Vol. III.* New York: Charles Scribner's Sons, 1969.

American Heritage. *Railroads in the Days of Steam.* New York: American Heritage Publishing Company, 1960.

Beard, Charles A. and Mary A. *America in Midpassage: Vol. V.* New York: The Macmillan Company, 1939.

Botkin, Benjamin, editor. *A Treasury of Railroad Folklore: The Stories, Tall Tales, Traditions, Ballads and Songs of the American Railroad Man.* New York: Crown Publishers, 1963.

Brown, Dee. *Hear That Lonesome Whistle*. New York: Holt, Rinehart & Winston, 1977.

Cook, F. P. *The American Struggle: The Story of the Continuing Conflict Between Labor and Management*. New York: Doubleday & Company, 1974.

Douglas, George H. *All Aboard: The Railroad in American Life*. New York: Paragon Press, 1992.

Dulles, Foster Rhea. *The United States Since 1865*. Ann Arbor: University of Michigan Press, 1969.

Ford, Henry Jones. *The Cleveland Era*. New Haven, Conn.: Yale University Press, 1919.

Litwack, Leon. *The American Labor Movement*. Englewood Cliffs, N.J.: Prentice-Hall, Inc., 1962.

Mumford, Lewis. *The City in History: Its Origins, Its Transformations, and Its Prospects*. New York: Harcourt, Brace, Jovanovich, 1961.

Tierney, Kevin. *Darrow: A Biography*. New York: T. Y. Crowell, 1979.

Welch, Richard E., Jr. *The Presidencies of Grover Cleveland*. Lawrence: University Press of Kansas, 1988.

Williams, John Hoyt. *A Great and Shining Road: The Epic Story of the Transcontinental Railroad*. New York: Times Books, 1988.

Index